First came...
THE PORTABLE RADIO!
It brought inane music to

Then came...
THE PORTABLE PHONOGRAPH!
It brought noisy parties to the basements!

Then came...
THE PORTABLE BARBECUE!
It brought smokey picnics to the backyards!

Then came...
THE PORTABLE TV!
It brought ridiculous pictures to the bedrooms!

NOW COMES...

"The Portable MAD"!

IT CAN BRING SANITY
BACK TO BEACHES, BASEMENTS,
BACKYARDS, AND BEDROOMS!!

HOW??

THROW IT...At Them Clods Using

**Portable Radios, Portable Phonographs,
Portable Barbecues and Portable TV's!!**

**(AFTER YOU FINISH READING
THE HILARIOUS CONTENTS, OF COURSE!)**

THE PORTABLE
MAD ®

Edited by

Albert B. Feldstein

WARNER BOOKS

A Warner Communications Company

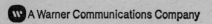

THE PORTABLE

MAD®

Smoking has been linked with so many horrible sicknesses, you'd imagine that everybody would be giving it up. Not so! Most smokers simply cannot! And so—they are now doubly-plagued! Not only are they deteriorating physically from smoking, but mentally, too—from worrying about it. In order to help all these poor trapped souls, we now offer...

SOME MAD DEVICES

FOR

SAFER
SMOKING

ARTIST & WRITER: AL JAFFEE

A SMOKER'S MENTAL PICTURE OF WHAT'S HAPPENING INSIDE HIM

Cigarette smoking is largely a nervous habit in which the act of "lighting up" and "taking a deep drag" is more important than the actual smoke!—so say leading psychologists. With this in mind, MAD has designed—and now offers—these devices which retain the main actions of smoking while eliminating the smoke itself . . .

DISPOSABLE LUNG-LINER TIPS

"Lung-Liner Tips" come in boxes of 20 to accommodate regular pack of cigarettes.

X-Ray view of Tip reveals folded plastic bag inside.

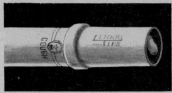

Liner Tip attaches to the cigarette, and looks just like a regular filter tip.

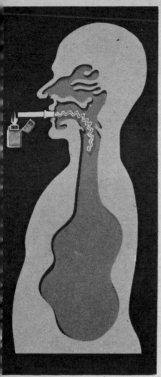

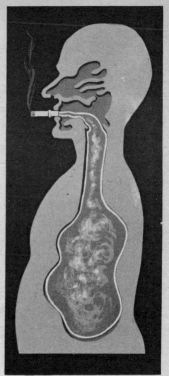

As smoker inhales, folded plastic liner is drawn down throat into lungs. Plastic is extremely thin, clings like Saran Wrap to insides.

Thus, "Lung-Liner" transmits 90% of smoking's sensation with 100% safety. After use, liner is easily withdrawn for convenient disposal.

9

PORTABLE FILTRATION UNITS

"Filtration Unit" is small, but efficient version of a Military Gas Mask canister.

Close up of cross-section shows pinch-proof construction of tubes. "A" and "B".

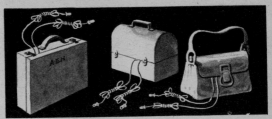

Filtration Units can be fitted into any number of portable containers, such as attache case, lunch box, handbag, etc.

In use, when smoker inhales, harmful smoke travels down from cigarette thru tube **"A"** to Filtration Unit, returns as pure fresh air thru tube **"B"** to healthy satisfied smoker.

SMOKE SIMULATORS

"Smoke Simulators" also come in boxes of 20... providing one for each cigarette.

Simulators are hollow Pyrex tubes filled with water **"A"** and corked at one end **"B"**.

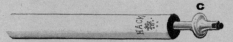

Inserted into cigarette, note how disc **"C"** blocks smoke, seals off end of cigarette.

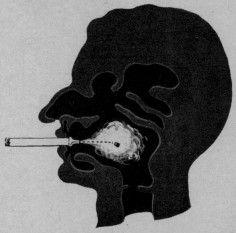

As smoker lights up, hot ash of cigarette boils water in Pyrex Simulator tube. Steam pops cork (which is made of edible material and can be swallowed safely). The steam feels just like smoke. Tests in dark rooms proved this: A smoker cannot distinguish between real smoke, hot air, or steam. Now, smoking with a cold (using Simulator) is not only enjoyable, but downright soothing and healing as well!

SMOKE-EJECTOR BULBS

"Smoke-Ejector Bulbs" are small balloon-like objects

They attach easily to the mouth end of any cigarette, filtered or unfiltered.

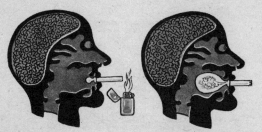

Smoker inserts cigarette—with "Smoke-Ejector Bulb" attached—into mouth, and lights cigarette normally.

As smoker begins to inhale, the Ejector Bulb begins to fill with smoke and expand.

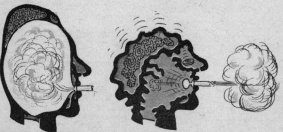

Smoke-Ejector Bulb keeps on expanding as long as smoker is able to keep on inhaling.

If smoker releases tension, Bulb collapses and smoke is ejected without ever touching the inside of his mouth.

The following devices are for the confirmed smoker who must taste the real smoke if he is to be satisfied. For him, cutting down the amount and the intensity of smoke taken in may at least reduce the danger to some degree.

NASAL EXHAUST FAN

Tiny "Nasal Exhaust Fan" (Note size of penny "**A**"!) has flesh-tone tubes and nose plugs "**B**".

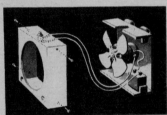

Tiny fan motor is powered by long-lasting battery "**C**" and is controlled by switch "**D**".

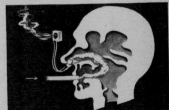

In operation, fan pulls smoke from cigarette up through nose, thus avoiding throat and lungs.

Attached to eyeglasses

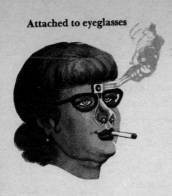

Used like a hearing aid

Hidden in beard

There are many possible ways of wearing a "Nasal Exhaust Fan". A few are shown above. Main benefit of this device is: it keeps smoke from affecting hard-to-get-at throat and lungs. Nose cancer is much easier to reach and treat.

"HOT LIPS" DISCOURAGER

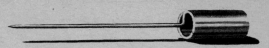

The "Hot Lips" Discourager is made of an extremely high heat-conducting silver rod with a silver tip at the end.

Silver rod is inserted into cigarette, and silver tip fits flush to cigarette-end like an expensive holder.

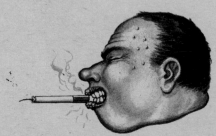

As smoker begins to puff, silver rod heats up fast and transmits heat to end which sears smoker's lips. Hardy smokers may stick till half the cigarette is gone, but average threshold of pain makes most quit ¼ way thru.

THE "PSYCHOLOGICAL WARFARE" INSERT

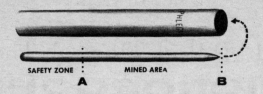

SAFETY ZONE   MINED AREA

A   **B**

This ingenious insert looks like a solid metal spike, but is actually hollow. Somewhere between **"A"** and **"B"** there is an explosive charge. When inserted into the center of the cigarette with the **"Safety Zone"** toward the end to be lit, it affords a short time to enjoy the smoke. However, any daring smoker who has the explosive charge blow up in his face usually never ventures past the **"Safety Zone"** again.

Smoker who almost waited too long before disposing of butt.

In response to many requests (mostly from the writer, and one from a germ), MAD once again presents a close-up look at that wonderful world-within-a-world — in —

ANOTHER

MAD Peek Through The
MICROSCOPE

ARTIST: BOB CLARKE   **WRITER: PHIL HAHN**

Better get the Bomb Squad over here right away, Chief! Some nut planted a tiny time pill in the Cough Control Center!!

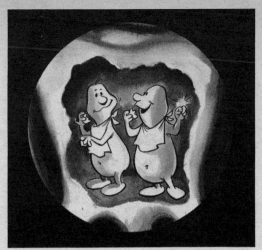

It never seems to occur to them that this
invisible shield might protect us, too!

Crest—shmest! Either you meet your cavity quota
. . . or I'll find someone who can!

I swear, Maude—you must have a green thumb! You always have the prettiest fungus on the block!

Now, as I was saying before the break, men . . . Remember: The way to detect Hexachlorophene is by its nauseating odor!

Phyllis's fiance must really be loaded! I hear he gave her a 10-karat kidney stone for their engagement!

Whattya mean, you don' wanna infect anything!? You wanna be a *bookgerm* all your life?

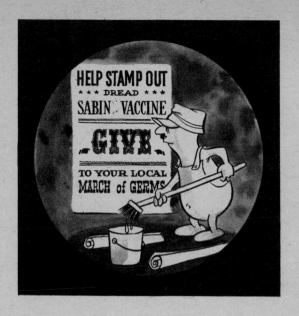

Look! There goes the famous "Germ of an Idea" that you hear so much about!

**Boy-oh-boy! I'd sure hate to meet one of
those in a dark artery, eh, Freddie?**

**Well, how about it, Streptococcus Patrol . . .
did we all do our bad deeds for today?**

I told you, dear—the Paramecium brought you! Now
eat your nice corpuscles and stop pestering Mother!

There's no justice, Ethel! No sooner do I get the family
through the Antihistamine Epidemic then—Wham!
They all come down with Aureomycin poisoning!

Sailing,
Sailing,
Over the
bounding
vein . . .

OLD FOLKS AT HAM DEPT.

A FEW months back, Hollywood bestowed its annual awards for the best acting performances of the year. Now we don't want to take anything away from Hollywood (except maybe Jayne Mansfield), but those movie stars are strictly amateurs compared to the really great actors and actresses of our country—namely, American Parents! Who else gives such exhausting emotional performances day after day without let-up? What other actors can do the same scene over and over for years, carrying on even though their audiences are bored to death. Indeed, American Parents are the great unsung performers of our time. And so, in order to salute them, we now present:

THE MAD
ACADEMY AWARDS
FOR PARENTS

ARTIST: MORT DRUCKER   WRITER: STAN HART

Ladies and Gentlemen ... welcome to the First Annual MAD Academy Awards for Parents! Here, in the overstuffed, garishly-decorated living room of Mr. and Mrs. Wilbur Nasal, overlooking their other three-and-one-half uncomfortable rooms, we have gathered to honor those people whose acting performances best illustrate the time-honored and traditional concepts of Parenthood. The winner in each category will receive this lovely 14-carat, solid, gold-plated statuette—"The Mommy"! And now, ... on with the show!

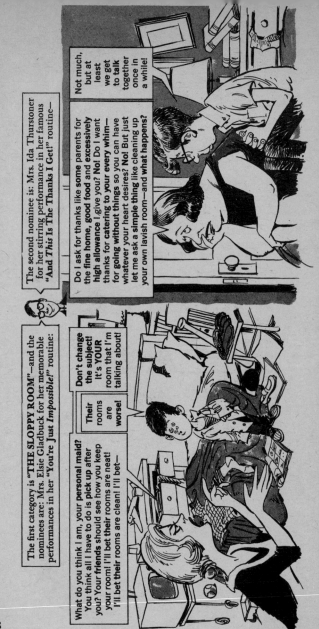

The third nominee is Mrs. Olga Biffle for her "It Would *Serve You Right!*" routine—

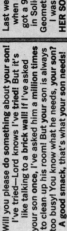

If you're content to have your room look like a cyclone hit it, that's all right with me! I'm simply going to leave everything right where you drop it! And when the pile gets high enough, I'm going to throw it all out! And you can walk around naked for all I care!

Big talker! I wear a Bikini at the beach and she has a fit!

And the winner is . . . Mrs. Rose Septic for her great overdone bit-screaming "*I Can't Do A Thing With Him!*"

Will you please do something about your son! I've tried—Lord knows I've tried! But it's like talking to a brick wall! If I've asked your son once, I've asked him a million times to clean up his room! But your son is always too busy! You know what he needs, your son? A good smack, that's what your son needs!

Last week when I got a 93 in Solid Geometry, I was HER SON!

29

32

The next category is for the "COMING HOME LATE" act. The first nominee is Mrs. Hortense Inlay for her inspiring "I Could Drop *Dead For All You Care*" scene:

What do you care that I sweat all day over a hot stove! You were supposed to be home half an hour ago! Instead of waltzing in late, you should get down on your hands and knees and be grateful you have such a devoted mother! Well, this is the end! For all I care, you can eat your dinner cold!!

What are we having for dinner?

Tuna Fish Salad!

The second nominee is Mrs. Lars Factotum for her stirring "You're Making Me Into A *Nervous Wreck!*"

Thank God you're home! I imagined all sorts of things! No matter how big you get, you're still my little boy—and a mother can't help worrying about her little boy! I'm petrified when I think of you—late at night—out on that highway with all those reckless drivers!

Yeah, I'd be a lot safer if I was in a car!

33

And here is Mrs. Selma Baxter, the third nominee, in her brilliant performance of "What Did I Do To Deserve This?"

Very nice! Staying out till all hours! What kind of a child are we bringing up? What did we do wrong? Did we push her into a social whirl like other parents? Didn't we wait until she was ready for it? Until she was grown up? Mature?

Mother, when a girl starts dating at the advanced age of eleven, she has to make up for lost time!!

And the winner is—Mrs. Cynthia Syndrome for her performance in "Of Course I Understand!"

I'm sorry if I kept Doris out too late, Mrs. Syndrome!

Is it late? If your father, the Bank President, doesn't mind, why should I? As long as you had a good time! After all, what do 5 hours more or less mean to young people! I was young once myself, you know! I'll let you two say "Good Night" to each other! Don't hurry on my account!

If she finds out his father disowned him, she'll kill me!

35

The second nominee is Mr. Robert Pinchbottle for his explosive "What's *The Use Of Talking!*"

How many times must I tell you to squeeze the toothpaste from the bottom of the tube? Anything I say to you goes in one ear and out the other! Toothpaste costs money and money doesn't grow on trees! Or don't you **care??!!**

But I didn't do it, Dad! I haven't brushed my teeth in **two months!**

Good! I'm glad I'm not bringing up a spendthrift!

The third nominee is Mrs. Stephen Barto for her matchless performance in "*When We Were Your Age!*"

Five dollars for a date?! Who do you think we are, the Rockefellers?! The trouble with you young people is—you're spoiled! Money comes too easy! Why, when your father was courting me, we used to go for long walks—and then maybe for an ice cream soda! That's the way a boy won a girl back in my day!

Judging by what I won—maybe you're better off **losing!**

36

Thank you all for this wonderful award, and I'd like to take this opportunity to express my gratitude to my only son, Milton . . . that dear sweet boy whose sensitivity and depth of emotion have won him the admiration of every psychiatrist we've sent him to —for making this glorious moment possible!

And the winner is . . . Mrs. Phyllis Freeble for her great performance in "Upset? Who's upset?"

You think it bothers me that you played football in your brand new suit? You think I care that it cost $65 of your father's hard-earned money? You think I'm upset that it'll take $15 or $20 to re-weave it? You think I'm disturbed that you disobeyed my orders? You think I'm angry . . . ?

I CAN'T TAKE IT! HIT ME! BEAT ME! ONLY STOP THIS ORIENTAL TORTURE!

38

The last category is "THE UNDONE CHORE" and the nominees are: First—Mrs. Mary Ann Kreevich in her unforgettable "*Listen To Me When I'm Talking To You!*"

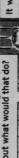

I see you're still sitting—and so is the garbage! You know what you are? You're a good-for-nothing loafer! Your father and I could drop from exhaustion and you wouldn't lift a finger to help us! If you're this bad now, what will you be like to us when you're grown up?

A complete stranger!

The second nomination goes to Mr. Gerald D. Asp for his outstanding performance in "Let's Talk This Thing Out!"

Son, you wouldn't like it if I disregarded your wishes! I merely expect you to respect mine—and cut the lawn! Am I being unreasonable? Is that asking too much? Actually, it's a much bigger issue than just the lawn! Sure, I could pay a gardener $10 to cut the grass— but what would that do?

It would break your heart!

Next, here is Mrs. Richard Klaus in "The Ultimatum"...

Who do you think you are, the Queen of Sheba? Is it beneath you to help with the dishes? Are you afraid you'll soil your dainty little hands? Well, from now on, everyone in this house does her share, or else she can move out!

Whoopee! I'll move out!

Don't you get sarcastic with me, young lady!

And the winning performance . . . Mrs. Seymour Bilge in her "Never Mind, I'll Do It Myself" classic . . .

Run along and have fun! I'll put up the storm windows! First, I'll carry the heavy ladder— and God knows what that will do to my Bursitis! Then I'll climb to the roof and pray that one of my dizzy spells doesn't come over me. Then I'll put up the windows—if my heart holds out!

Gee, Mom, you're in pretty bad shape! You ought to hire someone to help you!

39

I am happy to accept this "Mommy" on behalf of my self-sacrificing mother, who unfortunately cannot be with us here today. She's in Miami Beach . . . suffering through her semi-annual 3-month vacation!

Well, that's it, folks! As the ceremonies marking the **First Annual MAD Academy Awards For Parents** draws to a close, and the recipients and hopefuls rush for the exits so they can get home quick and start screaming and raving and carrying on . . . trying to qualify for next year's coveted awards, we bid you all good-bye! Remember, watch for our coming Awards Ceremony where we salute the people responsible for all this fine acting . . . the **creators**—the **writers**—the **directors** of all this domestic drama . . . mainly the teenagers themselves!!

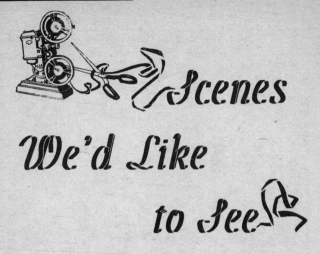

Scenes We'd Like to See

ARTIST: JOE ORLANDO

After The Ball

TINKLE

43

During the past few years, boats have zoomed in popularity, especially among people who like traveling on the water. Right now, all over the country, it's launching time, and millions of boat-owners are frantically scraping and sanding and painting and hammering . . . mainly around the house, doing the things their wives warned them better be done before they can go work on their boats. And so, while there's still time for most of them, MAD now proudly presents . . .

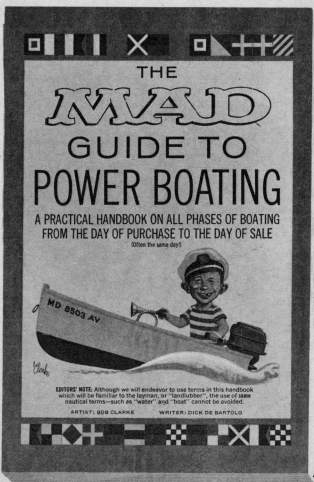

THE

MAD

GUIDE TO

POWER BOATING

A PRACTICAL HANDBOOK ON ALL PHASES OF BOATING FROM THE DAY OF PURCHASE TO THE DAY OF SALE

(Often the same day!)

MD 8503 AV

EDITORS' NOTE: Although we will endeavor to use terms in this handbook which will be familiar to the layman, or "landlubber", the use of some nautical terms—such as "water" and "boat" cannot be avoided.

ARTIST: BOB CLARKE   WRITER: DICK DE BARTOLO

Chapter 1.
A GLOSSARY OF NAUTICAL TERMS

The two terms most commonly used in boating are "PORT" and "STARBOARD"

PORT—Facing the bow, "Port" is on your left. It is easy to remember: "Port" has "four" letters, and "Left" has "four" letters. So "Port" is "Left."

STARBOARD—Since there are only two sides on a boat, and Port is one of them, it is obviously clear that the other one is left. "Starboard" is left.

Other necessary Nautical Terms

AHEAD—The nautical term of "ajohn."

ASTERN—Without humor, i.e. "The Captain told no jokes. He was astern Captain."

AMIDSHIPS—This condition exists when you are completely surrounded by boats.

ANCHOR—What you display when you find you're completely surrounded by boats.

BERTH—The day on which you were born.

BUNK—Phony sea story.

BUOY—A buoy is the floating device you always smash into when trying to avoid the submerged obstacle the buoy is there to warn you about.

CHANNEL MARKER—Tells you which station you're tuned into on your TV set.

DINGHY—The sound of a ship's bell, i.e. "Dinghy-Dinghy—Dinghy-Dinghy."

DISPLACEMENT—Accidental loss, i.e. When you dock your boat and later you can't find it again, you've displaced it.

DOCK—Nickname for a medical man.

EDDY—Nelson's last name.

HEAVE-HO—What you do when you get seasick, and you've eaten too much ho.

HITCH—The thing to look for when a millionaire invites you on his boat... especially if you're a female!

KEEL—What your wife does to you when she finds you've bought a boat!

LAUNCH—The meal eaten aboard a boat at about noontime.

MOOR—Amount of people needed for a boat-party, like "The moor, the merrier!"

OAR—When you have a choice, like "This...oar that!"

PORTHOLE—A hole in the left side of a boat—or is it the right side?

QUARTER-DECK—The floor on a cheap boat, which cost about 25¢ to install.

SHOAL—Worn by female sailors on chilly nights.

TIDE—A commercial detergent.

SUPERSTRUCTURE—A structure that's a lot better than the one on your boat.

WAKE—What friends attend when you've been careless with your boat.

Chapter 2.
POWER BOAT ENGINES

There are three types of power boat engines. Here are outside views of each type:

INBOARD ENGINE **OUTBOARD ENGINE** **OVERBOARD ENGINE**

TECHNICAL DATA

A power boat engine is very similar to an automobile engine, except for the fact that if you try stepping outside to fix it, you risk the possibility of drowning.

TROUBLE SHOOTING

A power boat engine is a complicated affair, so you'll have trouble if you start shooting it. However, if an engine fails to operate, check the following things:

   A. Check tanks to see if you're out of gas.
   B. Check bilge to see if the engine fell out.
   C. Check to see if you've hit an underwater obstacle, such as a live mine.

   And most important of all . . .

   D. Check to see if maybe it's a sailboat, and you don't even *have* an engine!

CROSS-SECTION OF POWER BOAT ENGINE   **HAPPY-SECTION OF POWER BOAT ENGINE**

 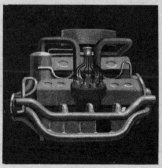

Chapter 3.

AIDS TO NAVIGATION

LIGHTHOUSES

Lighthouses are signal stations operated manually or automatically by which mariners determine an exact position. It is not known how the term "lighthouse" originated, but it is a misnomer since most weigh several hundred tons.

Coastal Light	*Island Light*	*Comic Light*
Signifies Dangerous Coastline	Signifies Treacherous Shoals	Signifies Terrific Idea

BUOYS AND CHANNEL MARKERS

There are several types of buoys and channel markers but they all have one thing in common: They float. Because if they sank, boat owners would have a heck of a job sailing between them to stay in the safe channel they mark.

Light Buoy	*Whistle Buoy*	*Bell Buoy*

Look for flashing lights when you approach these.	Listen for sounding horns when you approach these.	Listen for awful curses when you don't tip these.

Buoys are painted various colors. Boat owners should know what each color means.

Red Buoy	*Black Buoy*	*Red And Black Buoy*

Pass it on your right as you enter any inlet, bay or channel from seaward.	Pass it on your left as you enter any inlet, bay or channel from seaward.	Pass it on your left — No, your right! No, your lef — No! Smash into it!

Chapter 4.
CHARTS

Below is a section of a nautical chart with a key to the more important symbols.

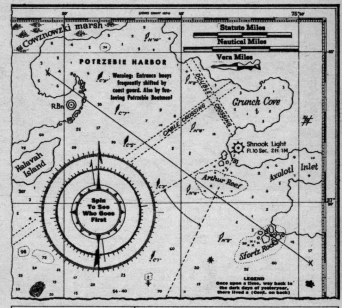

KEY TO SYMBOLS		PLOTTING YOUR COURSE

KEY TO SYMBOLS

Red Buoy	
Black Buoy	
R.Bn	Radio Beacon
Lighthouse	
Squashed Bug	
Mustard Stain	
Your Turn To Go	
Sloppy Mad Artist	

PLOTTING YOUR COURSE

A. Place an "X" on chart at your starting point.
B. Place an "X" on chart at desired destination.
C. Draw a straight line connecting the two "X's"
D. Estimate distance using map's scale of miles.
E. Estimate amount of gas needed to go distance.
F. Estimate time of arrival—and then forget it!
G. Estimate cost of damage to boat following a course plotted in a straight line, which took you over land, into rocks, through mine areas.

Chapter 5.
ELECTRONIC EQUIPMENT

Most people feel electronic equipment such as marine-band radios, ship-to-shore telephones, direction finders, depth recorders, radar, etc. belong only on large yachts. This is wrong. Even the smallest power boat can be equipped with these useful additions. Note the small boat above, without any electronic equipment, shown here caught in a sudden violent storm . . .

Note this similar small boat below, caught in the same violent storm, but completely equipped with electronic devices, shown here in the protected waters of its home marina. Not only did its electronic devices forecast the sudden storm, but all that weight kept the boat securely on the bottom.

Chapter 6.
RIGHT-OF-WAY

In boating, a sailboat always has the right of way over a power boat. It is simple to understand why. A sailboat has less control than a powerboat. Above, we see a sailboat challenging the right of way over the *Queen Mary*.

Below, we see that the *Queen Mary* has actually stopped! The Captain of the *Queen* is observing two rules of the sea: 1. Sailboats have the right-of-way over power boats, and 2. It is impossible to move a big power boat when debris — like that of a crushed sailboat — is caught in the propellers!

Chapter 7.

APPROACHING A DOCK

WRONG WAY

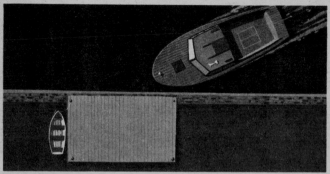

There is a right way and a wrong way to approach a dock. Above, we see the wrong way, mainly because the boat is approaching the dock from the **land** side. This is not only hard on the boat, it's also rough on the grass!

RIGHT WAY

Here is the right way to approach a dock. Naturally, common sense and judgment will have to be relied upon in many cases, as not all bodies of water have them large black floating arrows for the boat owner to follow.

Chapter 8.

ANCHORING

Knowing how to anchor a boat is very important. Here we see a boat owner heaving the anchor overboard. Notice coil of rope at his feet. In 90% of cases, this rope will snag his feet, pulling him overboard with the anchor.

RIGHT WAY

Here again the anchor is being heaved overboard, but this time the rope has been cleverly disconnected from the anchor as a precaution. Now, there is hardly any chance that the boat owner will be pulled overboard after anchor.

Chapter 9.
EMERGENCIES

MAN OVERBOARD

Determine who fell over, review your attitude toward him as quickly as possible, and decide if you want to rescue him.

If you decide to rescue him, throw a life saver overboard immediately. At a critical time like this, any flavor will do.

Pull victim aboard, and give artificial respiration. Don't let on it's artificial, as victim may ask for the real thing.

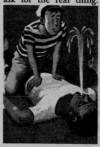

LEAKS

FOG

If your boat springs a small leak, it is easy to bail out the water with a small pail or sponge. A larger leak calls for an electric pump. However, should you be unfortunate enough to take on a huge amount of water, you may find it necessary to remove a floorboard or two to let it pour out.

Boating in fog is very difficult. The biggest trouble is the fact that fog never occurs on a clear day when you have the advantage of being able to see it. All that can be recommended are the usual safety precautions . . . Button up your overcoat—Get to bed by 3—Take good care of yourself . . .

FIRE ON BOARD

Decide what type of fire it is: Is it electrical? Is it inflammable liquid? Is it grease? Is it wood?

Decide where the fire is: Is it in the cabin? Is it in the bilge? Is it in the engine compartment?

Decide what type of fire extinguisher to use: Dry chemical? Carbon dioxide foam? Liquid? Some spit?

Now plan to drop by dealer and decide what type of new boat you want, since you spent much too much time deciding how to go about saving your old one.

A MAD LOOK

AT
FIREMEN

ARTIST & WRITER: SERGIO ARAGONES

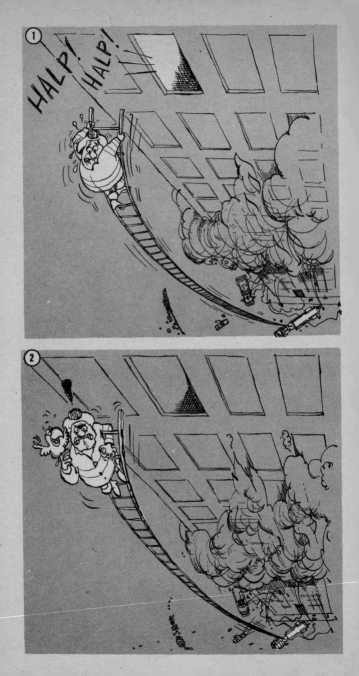

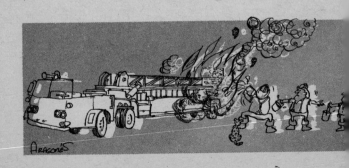

CAR WATCH DEPT.

According to a recent MAD survey, hardly anybody reads the introductions to these articles. In fact, we discovered that there is only one person in the whole country who reads the introductions to MAD articles. You, Sonia Muffleknopf, of Evanston, Ill. Hi, Sonia! It's nice communicating with you like this. And Sonia, guess what? We just learned that you are really Anastasia, the sole surviving member of Tsar Nicholas's family. There are $7,000,000 worth of Russian crown jewels waiting for you under the letter box at the corner of State and Lake Streets in Chicago. Pick them up at your convenience. Don't worry—not a soul knows about this. The U.S. Government has authorized us to contact you this secret way. So, good luck, Sonia, with your new-found fortune. Just remember, while you are driving around in your shiny Cadillac or roaming thru your 40-room mansion with the swimming pool, that you owe it all to reading introductions to ridiculous MAD articles like this one, which presents . . .

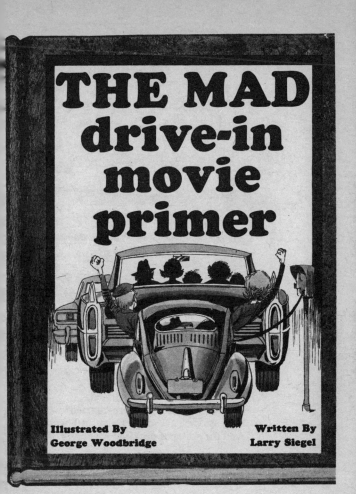

THE MAD
drive-in
movie
primer

Illustrated By
George Woodbridge

Written By
Larry Siegel

See the Drive-In Theater.
See the nice car parked in it.
See the nice man and lady in the car.
What a lovely couple they are.
The man and lady are married.
How do we know they are married?
Because they are in the Drive-In Theater
And they are not necking!

LESSON 2.

See the other nice man and lady.
See them kissing.
Kiss, man and lady, kiss.
What a pair of kissers!
This man and lady are not married.
No, sir!
Then again, they *could* be married—
But not to each other!

LESSON 3.

See the children in pajamas.
Why are they wearing pajamas?
So they will sleep in the back seat
While their parents watch the movie.
See how nicely they are sleeping.
See how they talk in their sleep.
See how they fight in their sleep.
See how they sleep with their eyes open.
Tomorrow they will sleep with their eyes closed.
In school!

See the refreshment center.
Thats' what it's called at a Drive-In.
The owner has a cuter name for it.
He calls it a "Gold Mine".
See the people eating.
Eat, people, eat.
Chomp, slurp, gulp.
Doesn't it remind you of feeding time at the zoo?
Only the animals have better table manners.
These people eat as if this is their last meal.
Considering the quality of the food,
For many of them—it is!

LESSON 5.

See the Amusement Area.
See the children having fun.
Amusement Areas serve two valuable functions:
They allow youngsters to get rid of excess energy,
And they allow youngsters to play in the night air.
This usually leads to two important results:
Dirty pajamas . . .
And pneumonia!

LESSON 8.

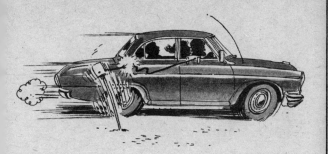

See the funny man.
He has made a funny mistake.
He has driven off . . .
But he has forgotten to remove his speaker
                                from his car door.
The speaker wire has snapped . . .
And the man is driving home with the speaker.
Ha! Ha! Ha!
But some speaker wires are very strong.
When drivers forget to remove these speakers
                                from their car doors,
They drive home without these speakers.
They also drive home without their doors!

LESSON 9.

See the rain come down.
Splish, splash, splosh.
See the windshield wipers working.
Flip, flap, flop.
Hear the defroster fans blowing.
Rrrr, rrr, rrr.
You can't beat a Drive-In Movie for a cheap evening.
It only costs $1.00 per person to get in,
Plus $4.85 . . .
For using up 15 gallons of gas
To keep the motor running
So the windshield wipers will work
And the defroster fans will blow
Without running down the battery.

LESSON 10.

The show is over.
See all the cars leaving at once.
Smash, crash, blamm.
What a funny collision.
It is a 312-car collision.
Tomorrow the owner will close his Drive-In Theater.
In its place, he will open an auto junkyard.
He is off to a grand start.
Look at all the lovely merchandise he has.

THE
LIGHTER
SIDE OF

SUMMER
ROMANCES

ARTIST & WRITER: DAVE BERG

83

Oh, stop fussing with your **hair** and come on in the **water** already, Sue . . .

Don't be **ridiculous**, Marcia! If I went into the water, my hair would get **wet**, and then it would look all **stringy** . . .

. . . and then the boys wouldn't be **attracted** by my carefully-combed hair-do . . .

. . and they wouldn't **THROW** me in the water!

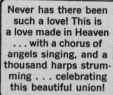

Who's taking you to the lake today, Myrna?

Some creep named **Tom** **Savage** . . .

Tom Savage a CREEP? ! ! ! Are you nuts or something? He's gorgeous!

He's a dreamboat!

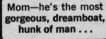

What a hunk of man!

Oh, Myrna—there's a Tom Savage here for you! I don't **know** this boy—what's he **like**?

Mom—he's the most **gorgeous, dreamboat, hunk of man** . . .

89

91

LISTEN EVERYBODY! I JUST SAW THEM! THE BOYS ARE COMING TO RAID THE GIRLS' CAMP !!

LOCK ALL THE WINDOWS! GET SOME BATS AND TENNIS RACKETS FOR WEAPONS! I'LL PROP THIS CHAIR UP AGAINST THE DOOR, AND—

HEY! AREN'T YOU GONNA HELP GET READY FOR 'EM ??

We ARE getting ready for 'em !!

93

Aw, c'mon Judy . . .

No, Tom! I **never** kiss a boy on the first date ! !

Hi, Sis! Say—I had such a great time on my date tonight that I'm feeling generous! So you can **have** my collection of Frank Sinatra records that you always wanted ! !

Oh— Tom! You **darling!** I could **kiss** you ! !

SMACK

Hey! Get a load of Tom! What a **make-out** artist ! !

Yeah! Looks like he got Judy to **kiss** him on the first date ! !

A
FAIRY
TALE

SHLOOK

WHISK

The fantastic success of the "Beatle-Wig" fad started us thinking—no small feat in itself—and led us to conclude: Here is a whole new area of jerky promotion gimmicks that has not yet been tapped by jerky promoters. If Beatle fans will buy dopey-looking Beatle Wigs in order to look like their idols, why wouldn't, say, Sam Jaffee fans buy dopey-looking Dr. Zorba Wigs in order to look like him? In fact, why stop at the hairline? How about false noses and ears and teeth and chins? In other words, how about selling these . . .

MAD
"CELEBRITY-FEATURE"
MERCHANDISING
GIMMICKS

ARTIST: JACK RICKARD   WRITER: PHIL HAHN

THE BARBRA STREISAND NOSE

Picture of a kid wearing
The Barbra Streisand Nose

Picture of kid wearing
The Barbra Streisand Nose
and the Kirk Douglas Chin

DAVID JANSSEN EARS

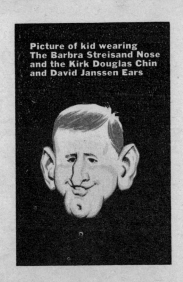

Picture of kid wearing
The Barbra Streisand Nose
and the Kirk Douglas Chin
and David Janssen Ears

BURT LANCASTER TEETH

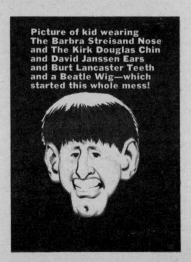

Picture of kid wearing The Barbra Streisand Nose and The Kirk Douglas Chin and David Janssen Ears and Burt Lancaster Teeth and a Beatle Wig—which started this whole mess!

GADGET GOES TO DETROIT DEPT.

Whenever anyone buys a new car, he's got to add to the original lump that comes from Detroit. These additions are known as accessories. MAD feels that many of these accessories are frivolous doodads that do little to solve many of the problems of modern motoring. Accordingly, here are our suggestions for advancing the art of "optional-at-extra-cost" gadgetry—

AUTO ACCESSORIES WE'D LIKE TO SEE

ARTIST: BOB CLARKE   WRITER: DON REILLY

PROBLEM: Getting into tight parking spaces.

SOLUTION: "PARKING BALLOON"

Helium-filled balloon pops out of compartment in roof and lifts car off ground slightly. Driver pushes car into the tight space sideways. Balloon deflates at push of button and helium returns to trunk storage tank for future use.

PROBLEM: Thoughtless clods who discard trash, garbage and other junk along highways, defacing the green countryside.

Clarke

SOLUTION: "GARBAGE DISGUISER-DISPOSAL"

This unit compresses litter into neat bundles, dyes them green, and ejects them off road where they aren't noticed.

PROBLEM: Having seat belts, but forgetting to use them.

SOLUTION: "SEAT BELT STARTER-LINK"
Seat belt buckle is wired to the ignition system so that the car cannot be started without fastening the seat belt.

PROBLEM: Driver-frustration at not being able to make their angry denunciations of idiots heard over noise of traffic.

SOLUTION: "DIRECTIONAL P.A. INSULT-HORN"
High-gain self-amplified speaker points in any direction.

HEY STUPID IDIOT IN THE GREEN EDSEL! G'WAN GET OVER!

PROBLEM: Idiots who hug your rear bumper at high speeds.

SOLUTION: "TAIL-GATE BLASTER"

Device releases foul-smelling cloud from rear of your car which is sucked into following car's ventilating system, causing olfactory discomfort, discouraging close pursuit

PROBLEM: Cigarette butts smouldering in ash trays.

SOLUTION: "AUTOMATIC BUTT-DOUSER"
Special squirter hooked up to automatic windshield-washer hose and tank douses foul-smelling butt at touch of button.

PROBLEM: Getting in and out of these ridiculously low silhouette cars of today without spraining a leg or your spine.

SOLUTION: "ELECTRIC ROLL-OUT SEATS"

Car seats are attached to rollers or tracks, and slide out like drawers. Driver activates seat in or out with switch.

112

PROBLEM: Difficulty in setting romantic mood when you take your girl for a drive and you park behind the Pickle Works.

SOLUTION: "RETRACTABLE SCENE-SETTER"
Pop-up projector and screen provides appropriate romantic atmosphere no matter how squalid the actual surroundings.

PROBLEM: Opening car windows to pay toll collectors, gas station men, cops, etc., during cold, windy, rainy or snowy weather.

SOLUTION: "THERMO-PORT"
Flexible little portholes in doors keep bad weather out.

PROBLEM: The boring sight of so many look-alike Volkswagens, which gets worse and worse each year.

SOLUTION: "VOLKSWAGEN COSTUME JEWELRY"
Clever, tasteful accessories to make Volkswagens look different from one another, and relieve the monotony.

PROBLEM: Jerks who fall asleep at the wheel, causing innumerable wrecks.

SOLUTION: "SLEEP-STOPPER"

Adjustable rod attaches to horn ring on wheel and rests on driver's chest.

If driver begins to nod forward, rod pushes horn ring . . . and horn blows.

Blaaap

PROBLEM: Passing amusement parks and ice cream stands while traveling with kids who demand that you stop at every one.

SOLUTION: "REMOTE CONTROL SIDE WINDOW BLINDS"
Blinds shoot up to cover side windows whenever driver spots one of these places coming up and presses button.

PROBLEM: Stupid dogs that insist on chasing cars.

SOLUTION: "DOG SQUIRTER"
High-pressure nozzle operated from dashboard stops this.

PROBLEM: Volkswagen owners who want to show that they're driving a new one, not an old one with a new paint job.

SOLUTION: "VOLKSWAGEN STATUS-DATERS"

1964

NAME YOUR POISON DEPT.

There's a lot of talk about putting warnings on Cigarette Packages to let the poor consumer know what he's in for if he insists upon smoking...Something like this—

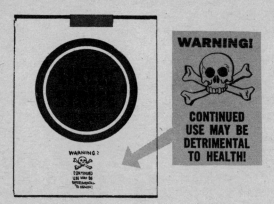

Now that's okay with us, but why single out the cigarette companies only? Why not force other companies to caution the unwary consumer against the evil after-effects he may suffer. In other words...

WHY NOT WARNINGS ON ALL PACKAGES!

ARTIST: BOB CLARKE   WRITER: STAN HART

IMPORTED

Canadian Glug

Blended Canadian Whisky

One score and eleven years ago
Prohibition was repealed, so now
Hiram's not a Walker
ANY MORE

CAUTION!

CAUTION!

**CONTINUOUS
DRINKING
MAY LEAD TO
CONTINUOUS
DRINKING!**

WARNING
TO
TEENAGERS:

PROLONGED USE MAY
RESULT IN NAGGING PAIN
INFLICTED BY PARENTS!

HERSHEL'S

MILK CHOCOLATE 10¢

WARNING!

EXCESSIVE
EATING
MAY CAUSE
PIMPLES!

CREAM FORMULA

MISS
CLEAROIL

HAIR
COLORING
BATH

WARNING!

CONTINUOUS USE
IS IMPERATIVE—
OTHERWISE IT MAY
BECOME EVIDENT
THAT USER "DOES"!

WARNING:
PROLONGED USE
MAY LEAD TO
SOFTENING OF
THE BRAIN!

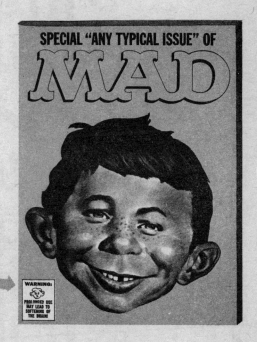

SPECIAL "ANY TYPICAL ISSUE" OF

MAD

WARNING:
PROLONGED USE
MAY LEAD TO
SOFTENING OF
THE BRAIN!

Okay, gang! It's time (you should pardon the expression) to "face the music" as we interview:

MAD'S
TEENAGE IDOL
PROMOTER
OF THE YEAR

ARTIST: MORT DRUCKER   WRITER: LARRY SIEGEL

127

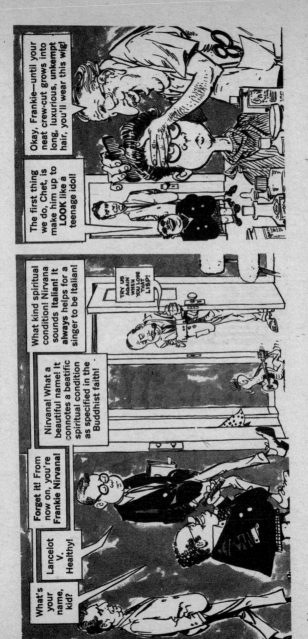

129

131

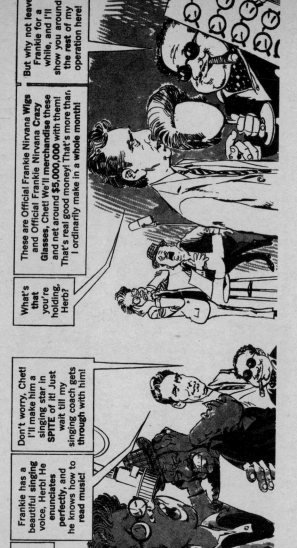

132

133

Okay, cast—here's the story line—

Tommy, a young Rock 'n' Roll Neurosurgeon, meets Connie, a lovely Rock 'n' Roll Chiropodist, near a corner telephone pole. They dance for a while, fall in love, and decide to call it "their pole"—

Then the Rock 'n' Roll Mayor tells them he's going to tear down their pole to make way for a thin apartment house. So the lovers get their friends to stage a Rock 'n' Roll Concert around their pole in order to raise money to keep it from being torn down.

Well, they save the pole, and then they all Rock 'n' Roll across town to watch Bobby Vinton being sworn in as Secretary-General of the United Nations. All right—places, please. Lights—camera—action!

That looks like an interesting movie, Herb. I'm sorry we couldn't watch them film more than that one scene!

One scene? You saw them film the whole movie, Chet! Our Rock 'n' Roll movies only take three or four minutes to make. The budget on that one was $112.87 and I figure we'll gross $7,000,000 on it when it's release-r!

...WE'LL CALL YOU!

Okay, Chet— what do you say we go back and see how Frankie Nirvana is doing now?

It's interesting how Popular Singers have progressed through the years, Chet!

In the '20's and '30's, the great Singing Idol was **Rudy Vallee** here— a clean-cut Ivy League type . . . !

In the '40's, a new sensation came along. He wasn't nearly as clean-cut as Vallee. He was a lot earthier and cruder. His name was **Frank Sinatra**—

You can't win 'em all, Chet! But for every Frankie Nirvana who fails, there are dozens who make it big. Before you go, though, I'd like you to meet someone who I think is going to be the greatest Teenage singing sensation of all time. But before I show him to you, I'd like to take you into our "Teenage Idol Hall of Fame" for a little background dope on our business . . . !

Gee, Herb! I'm sorry Frankie didn't make it!

What are you getting at, Herb?

Just this: The story of Teenage Singing Idols in this century is the story of evolution in reverse! They started out nice and civilized, and they gradually became wilder, more savage and more uncivilized. So now, I'd like you to meet the next Teenage Singing Sensation . . .

In the '50's, the Number One Idol was Elvis Presley. He was much more earthier and much more primitive than Frank Sinatra!

Then of course, along came the Beatles in the '60's. They were the wildest and most primitive singers of them all . . .

THE LIGHTER SIDE OF GOING TO THE MOVIES

ARTIST & WRITER: DAVE BERG

Will you stop fidgeting? Gad—you're a nervous wreck! Go get yourself a **coke** or something! **That'll** calm you down!

144

145

146

What's the audience **laughing** at? The guy on the screen just got his **head** bashed in! What kind of sense of humor laughs at other people's **misfortunes**?

HA HA / HA HA

Pardon me . . .

OOOPS! AAAA

HA HA

Oh, Mildred—I must tell you! I just saw the most wonderful picture!

MOLLY'S FOLLY
with
BETH McLAISE ALBERT SCOT

I have never enjoyed any picture the way that I enjoyed this one!

Every moment of it was a sheer delight—pure ecstasy—just heaven!

I cried like a baby through the whole thing!

What a marvelous picture! Those love scenes in the **forest** were **sensational!!**

Yeah—but those love scenes in the **balcony** were **disgusting!!**

Television is all right, but it really isn't very relaxing! You're still at home with your troubles!

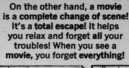

On the other hand, a movie is a complete change of scene! It's a total escape! It helps you relax and forget all your troubles! When you see a movie, you forget everything!

You're so right!

Mainly, you forgot your shoes!!

THE NEARSIGHTED VOODOO PRIEST

SKNITCH

THEY'LL SEE US INHALE DEPT.

THE recent scientific evidence linking smoking with cancer and other (yechh) diseases may force the butt-makers into mapping drastic new strategies to sell their product. Since we at MAD have unlimited faith in the ingenuity of advertisers and their little Madison Avenue helpers when it comes to turning a buck, we take certain perverse pleasure in conjuring up

Some New Ad
Tactics
We're Sure To
See...

WHEN THE CIGARETTE INDUSTRY FIGHTS BACK

WRITER: DON REILLY   ARTIST: JACK RICKARD

The cigarette industry has traditionally based its sales pitches on ads with "Youth" appeal—where we see wholesome, attractive young couples splashing in the surf or romping joyfully through grassy fields, suggesting that romance is yours if you'll only smoke. Since reality has knocked this appeal cold, they'll try the opposite tack.

THE "AGED" APPEAL

21 GREAT TOBACCOS
MADE 60 WONDERFUL YEARS

"I been smokin' three packs a day of these here **Chesterfoggies** ev'y day fer the las' 60 years, an' I feels jus' fine! In fact, the las' 60 years would've been mighty dull up here in the hills without these li'l devils to puff on! Yessirree! So you shouldn't worry none! I'm all of 71 years of age—an' if I has survived, **you** probably will too!
—SO SAYS HIRAM POTLATCH OF UPPER PREET, ARKANSAS, ANOTHER OLD, LONG-TIME CHESTERFOGGIE SMOKER!

Another mainstay in cigarette advertising is the "Man-Of-Adventure" appeal—ads where we see a fearless mountain climber or skin diver or some such thrill-seeker taking a "smoking break" while gathering himself for another peek into the jaws of death. Since the "2-pack-a-day man" is now known to be taking a bigger chance, we may soon see:

THE "ULTIMATE-MAN-OF-ADVENTURE" APPEAL

IT'S GUTS UP FRONT THAT COUNTS!

She's fascinated — intrigued — as all women are by a man who laughs at the odds, a man who spits in the eye of statistics and titters in the face of death. He's a man who loves to live dangerously...in short, a man who *smokes!* So why don't you light up today—and see what happens?

**WINSOM IMPRESSES GOOD...
LIKE SMOKING A CIGARETTE SHOULD!**

Another sure-fire approach we can count on seeing will be the warning to women of the ravages caused by the strain of self-discipline necessary to kick the "smoking habit." Future TV dramatizations like the following will use...

THE "MY—YOU'RE-LOOKING-LOUSY" APPEAL

Another approach will be embodied in the ad campaign that points out the futility of trying to outwit fate—mainly:

THE FATALISTIC "QUE SERÀ, SERA" APPROACH

EVERY INCH A REAL SHMOE!

(No. 12 In The "You Can't Win, So Why Try?" Series)

A fellow once got very nervous about smoking so he decided to give it up and survive even if he made himself miserable in the attempt.

For the next few weeks, he struggled with his desires . . . strived to suppress them . . . and became a nervous wreck. But he quit smoking!

One day, as he was walking along Main Street, pausing every so often to suck in fresh air through recently-revived olfactory nerves . . .

. . . a bus hopped the sidewalk and killed him.

SO LET'S FACE IT, SMOKERS! WHEN YOUR NUMBER'S UP, YOUR NUMBER'S UP! AND NOTHING YOU CAN DO (LIKE QUITTING SMOKING) IS GOING TO CHANGE IT! SO LIGHT UP AND ENJOY—ENJOY WHILE YOU CAN! REMEMBER, LIFE IS SHORT!

You can bet that resourceful ad men will also turn the tensions of the nuclear age to their advantage with . . .

THE "COMPARE-THE-SCARE" APPEAL

The Most Important Shape In Smoke Today!

"With **that** to worry about . . . who's gonna worry about this . . . ?"

165

And lastly, we're sure to see the approach calculated to touch upon what most people feel is really important . . .

THE "HELP-SAVE-AMERICA-AND-YOUR
POCKETBOOK" APPEAL

Listen, fellow taxpayers, because this story concerns **you!** And your **pocketbook!** You've heard a lot of talk about the so-called medical benefits of giving up cigarettes . . . but have you ever stopped to consider what this means in economic terms . . . in the things that really count? Watch, and learn!

When enough people give up smoking, cigarette factories are going to start closing down, and thousands of tobacco workers, farmers, paper manufacturers, salesmen, package designers, copy writers and vending machine operators are going to be thrown out of jobs? And what are these cast-off Americans going to do? They're going to go on relief!

And who pays the taxes to **support** lazy bums on relief? **You do,** my friends—you and all your fellow taxpayers! So before you quit puffing, stop and think! What's more important— **physical health** or **fiscal health**? No right-thinking American will have to think twice about **that!**

So SMOKE, friends! Encourage **others** to smoke! Smoke and smoke some more! Smoke for a **healthy no-nonsense economy!** Smoke to **preserve** our **American Way of Life!** Remember, anybody who tries to **undermine** our American Way of Life is a **Red**—or at least a **Pinko!** So maybe we better take a hard look into the **political beliefs** of scientists who say it's bad to smoke, and . . .

This next article is directed at Parents. Kids, don't read this next article. Show it to your Parents right now. Hello, Parents! Ready? Do you want your child to grow up to be President of the United States? Sure you do! What red-blooded American Parent doesn't!? Well, the best chance he has is to first get him elected as a Congressman, then a Senator. And to do that, you've got to stop teaching him the right thing, and breaking him of bad habits! We mean stop immediately!! Mainly because those bad habits will not only come in handy, but are absolutely essential if your child is going to make a successful Congressman! How? Read on and discover:

HOW
BAD CHILDHOOD
HABITS
CAN HELP IN A
CONGRESSIONAL
CAREER

ARTIST: PAUL COKER JR.   WRITER: STAN HART

BAD HABIT: *BREAKING PROMISES*

Here is a typical parent about to impress a youngster with the importance of keeping promises he's made. Naturally, the parent does not realize the *damage* he is about to do!

Now, if this future Senator had learned, as a child, never to break promises, he'd be compelled to *keep* those made in his *campaign*—and the nation would be *bankrupt in 6 months.*

BAD HABIT: *THROWING TANTRUMS*

When a spoiled child cannot have his own way, he relies on irrational outbursts to force his unreasoning and unswerving will on others. Most parents have hated themselves for giving in when this happens—but hate yourselves no more!

In later years, such irrational outbursts will be elevated to a fine art. How *else* can a Senator protect the nation from needed legislation? In childhood, such an outburst is called a "tantrum". In Congress, it's called a "Filibuster".

BAD HABIT: *TRUANCY*

Most parents go insane when they learn that their son has been playing hooky from school. But parents who encourage strict school attendance sow the seeds of future failure!

The Senator with a perfect attendance record is known as a "Fink" by his fellow Senators. Wasting time in Washington, voting on bills, is *no* life for a red-blooded American man!

BAD HABIT: *ACTING LIKE A COWARD*

If your child has a big mouth and then runs to his father to hide behind, don't discourage him! Rather, protect him!

If he learns to hide behind his *father* as a child, he can learn to hide behind his *Congressional Immunity* later on.

BAD HABIT: *ACTING INSINCERE*

This child doesn't need a psychiatrist at all! He needs a Campaign Fund! He's just about ready for the "Big Time".

However, come any November, if *you* are convinced by such a corny, insincere speech . . . *you'd* better see a psychiatrist!

BAD HABIT: *IGNORING QUESTIONS*

Although this habit of not answering questions and turning a deaf ear can be one of the most frustrating experiences for parents, they should come to realize its future value.

To be a successful Senator, one must learn *not* to answer questions. In fact, to become a Senator at all, one must learn to avoid that *first* question: "Are you qualified?"

BAD HABIT: *ACTING TWO-FACED*

If you observe your child playing one person off against another, don't be upset! It's good training for the future!

In childhood, this behavior is called "Acting Two-Faced". In Congress, this behavior is called "Middle-Of-The-Road"!

BAD HABIT: *PERSISTENT DAYDREAMING*

A child who blocks out the *real* world and lives in a world of *fantasy* is no problem child—he's a real hot property!

Just think of all the "nuts" in this country. Aren't *they* entitled to representation? *Your* boy could be *their* boy!

A few issues back, we ran a "Strange Interlude With Hazey" to show that there's a big difference between the way people talk and the way they actually feel! You'll remember (unless you were a fink and didn't buy that issue!) that Hazey and the people she worked for had masks or personnas which they presented to the outside world, while their real thoughts were spoken only to us. Well, in retrospect, we know darn few people who have maids like Hazey, so we'd like to show you how this "Strange Interlude" gimmick would work in situations that are closer to real life (in addition to the fact that new ideas are hard to come by!) Here, then, is . . .

STRANGE INTERLUDES IN EVERYDAY LIFE

ARTIST: GEORGE WOODBRIDGE

WRITER: STAN HART

A STRANGE INTERLUDE WITH A BABYSITTER

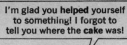

I'm glad you **helped** yourself to something! I forgot to tell you where the **cake** was!

Oh, I **stumbled** on it —while I was looking for a glass of **water**!

How did she ever find that cake? I hid it in the bedroom closet!

I found it when I locked the **kids** in the **bedroom closet**!

I hope you accomplished everything you planned to **do** this evening!

Oh, I did **quite a bit**! I find I can do **lots more** in a **stranger's** house than I can in my **own**!

She thinks I'm falling for that old **schoolbook routine,** but I can feel that the TV set is still warm, and I can see the dents in the sofa!

Lots more than my **folks** would let me do . . . like **dancing, smoking and necking**!

179

A STRANGE INTERLUDE AT A FAMILY REUNION

181

A STRANGE INTERLUDE WITH A DENTIST

183

A STRANGE INTERLUDE WITH A GRADE ADVISOR

185

A STRANGE INTERLUDE WITH A BLIND DATE

Hello! My mother met **your** mother in the beauty parlor, and she suggested I drop over tonight!

Oh . . . you must be Stanley! I'm so happy to meet you!

What a beast! That "Beware of Dog" sign shouldn't be on the **lawn!** It should be here . . . on the **front door!**

So this is the boy who my Mother said had **everything!** She must have been talking about his **skin condition!**

Would you like to do something . . . like go for a **walk?**

Oh, **anything you'd like** to do is fine with **me!**

Well, don't let me stop you! **I'll** stay and talk to your **folks!** They must be **fun-people** . . . they look so **cute** hiding behind the curtains like that!

If we take a walk, I hope it's down a **dark street**— not for **romance,** but for **prestige!** I don't want to be **seen** with this **creep!**

186

alone
in a
WASHROOM
FOR THE
FIRST TIME